COME ALIVE

CREATE YOUR RICHER, HAPPIER LIFE

BOOK ONE

Come Alive

Create Your Richer, Happier Life

CORALEE KULMAN

For permission requests, write to the publisher, addressed "Attention: Permissions Coordinator," at the address below.

admin@ThePublishingCircle.com
or
THE PUBLISHING CIRCLE, LLC
Regarding: Coralee Kulman
4615 NE 25th Court
Vancouver, WA 98663

The Publisher is not responsible for the Author's website, other mentioned websites, or content of any website that is not owned by the Publisher.

COME ALIVE—CREATE YOUR RICHER, HAPPIER LIFE / Coralee Kulman
FIRST EDITION
ISBN 978-1-947398-48-1 (PAPERBACK)
ISBN 978-1-947398-80-1 (LARGE PRINT)
ISBN 978-1-955018-00-5 (HARDCOVER)
ISBN 978-1-955018-06-7 (eBOOK)

DISCLAIMERS: This book is not intended as a substitute for the medical advice of physicians or psychological advice of therapists. It is made available with the understanding that neither the author nor the publisher is engaged in presenting specific medical, psychological, emotional, sexual, or spiritual advice. Nor is anything in this book intended to be a diagnosis, prescription, recommendation, or cure for any specific kind of medical, psychological, emotional, sexual, or spiritual problem. Each person has unique needs. This book cannot take those individual differences into account. The reader should regularly consult a licensed physician or therapist in matters relating to his/her physical or mental health.

The Author and Publisher made every effort to ensure the accuracy of the information within this book was correct at time of publication. Neither the Author nor Publisher assumes, and thereby disclaims, any liability to any part for any loss, damage, or disruption caused by errors or omissions, whether such errors or omissions result from accident, negligence, or any other cause.

Book design by Michele Uplinger

Come Alive—

Create Your Richer, Happier Life

Know the Unknown,
See the Unseen,
Feel the Unfelt,
Speak the Unspoken,
Hear the Unheard,
and
Find the True You
Alive and Well

Praise for Coralee Kulman

"Coralee has been instrumental to me on the road to both healing old wounds and in helping me through my journey towards finding what I truly want in life. She is direct, compassionate, intuitive and knowledgeable. I would highly recommend her services to anyone who is ready to move past their pain and unlock their infinite potential. With Coralee's guidance you can prepare yourself for mind-blowing insights and a newfound hope for the future."

JOHANNA MOELLER

"Coralee is such a beautiful soul! She helped me bring light to my darkness. I have learned to love the little things about myself and I never thought that was possible! Coralee truly has a gift.

KELSY KIMLE

"Coralee gave me the tools to use to remember who I am and what the qualities I love about me are (I honestly didn't think I really loved myself like that) . . . I literally had an AHA moment and was so surprised and overjoyed with my realization and acceptance of what I discovered. Coralee has a wonderful presence, safe space, and simple gestures. As I type this review I can feel my heart expand and my eyes tear up because I am truly happy and feel so light and loved. Thank you Coralee."

JULIA WHITE
REIKI PRACTITIONER

"Coralee Kulman is definitely someone who was born to help people. Her aura, her patience her whole demeanor just projects peace and you can talk endlessly to her and with her."

JANET LEON

"Working with Coralee has allowed me to look to the future, set goals, achieve those goals, and leave the past in the past. I have been able to learn from my past, realize what parts of it serve me and what parts no longer do. Coralee has been instrumental in my learning what a boundary is, setting boundaries and keeping boundaries. Coralee is that person that you can open up to, talk and cry with and create a new path."

HOLLY ANDERSON
OWNER, FIRMLY PLANTED REFLEXOLOGY

"I have worked with Coralee for a year or more and from the first time I met her I could feel her warmth, love and the kindness she had to offer. She warmed my heart with her gentle spirit and shared her insights, knowledge, and wisdom so gracefully! Sometimes she put my soul at ease, and at other times made me see that big nasty issues can be wonderful because it makes change happen and we can celebrate that! I love her way of guiding you to the truth you find inside yourself. I also really love her recap emails that you get after every session that will remind you in detail of what was talked about. This is outstanding and I can't believe she can remember it all with such detail . . . amazing!

JENNI WOLFE
CERTIFIED PERSONAL TRAINER / PILATES INSTRUCTOR

"Coralee is a rockstar! I have never met anyone who can change your perspective on something for the better! Whether it is something you have going on with your personal life or with your business, Coralee is a great resource!"

MATT VERTREES

"I am just blessed to have Coralee in my life. Her ability to help pinpoint my triggers and how to reflect, investigate, and overcome those triggers is amazing. Coralee's approach is different than any other I have experienced. She provides detailed feedback after every meeting and suggests realistic tools to implement to help one overcome obstacles. Imagine feeling vulnerable AND safe amidst your most deep rooted issues! Coralee is an absolute gem!"

ANGIE TAYLOR

"From the first day I met Coralee, I realized we had a true connection. She truly makes you feel safe, understood, and vaued as a person no matter what or where you are in your life. She was immediately able to give me constructive feedback about some issues I was dealing with, and helped encourage me to find my voice again! I would recommend Coralee to anyone looking to *"Come Alive"* again, and to live life feeling loved and valued . . . and to begin writing "your own story" for the rest of your life."

SUE LLEWELLYN

"Coralee Kulman is enchanting, to say the least. Her methodical and impeccable way of listening, speaking and coaching appears as if she is waving a "magic wand" and *poof,* what seemed a reality for years transforms. She has made an incredible difference to me."

SANDI GREEN

"Coralee is a fantastic life coach. She is so kind and caring. Being a Certified Practitioner of Neuro-Linguistic Programming, Coralee was able to skillfully guide me in developing my inner detective so I could get to the root of the problems quickly and resolve them. I'm so grateful for her."

HEIDI MOSS

"Coralee has definitely found her life's calling with her coaching business! She has such a calm, caring attitude and seems to know exactly what is needed for her coachees. I highly recommend her for any sort of coaching need."

RUTH FENN

"Coralee has a gentle and kind way in assisting an individual through emotional traumas. She accepted me unconditionally when I was transitioning though a difficult phase of my life. She reminded me that it was okay to feel everything I was feeling and to let everything flow out. Her guidance was not invasive, but flexible in application. I would recommend her
to anyone looking to "sift through the rubble" to find the value in their life experiences, and shift to a healing perspective."

A SWEET, BEAUTIFUL SOUL
WHO WOULD LIKE TO REMAIN ANONYMOUS

"I can't even begin to explain what Coralee's coaching has done for my life! From relationships, to the loss of a 15-year career, financials, goals, and working through the myriad issues of childhood abuse and the emotions and lack of self-worth that accompanies all of that mess. In just my second one-on-one session with Coralee, we were able to start tackling those "blank" spots and rewire how I not only see myself, but my life as a whole. She helped me tap into my passion of working with others and her support and mentorship has been endless! Coralee will forever be my life coach.

HEATHER HANSON

Dedication

This book is dedicated to my husband, Lance, who has been my biggest supporter. It is humbling to have such a wonderful man in my life who has so much faith in me.

Table of Contents

INTRODUCTION

Why Come Alive in Creating a Richer, Happier Life?

"Coming alive is living a life that's more satisfying than your wildest dreams could ever conceive. Go wild, go big, go for the brass ring, and Come Alive. Then be ready to see your life change into something marvelous."

CORALEE KULMAN

Ever Wish You Could Change Your Life?

- Do you sometimes feel stuck and don't know what to do?
- Are you feeling overwhelmed because your life seems so complex?
- Ever felt like you could have done better in life if you had made different choices?
- Do you feel overwhelmed when you face a new

challenge?

- Is it hard for you to focus on what you want?
- Do you sometimes react emotionally and then regret it?
- Are there habits that seem to get in your way that you can't seem to change?
- Do you want to find the answers to *all* your questions?
- Would you like to see how your unconscious childhood memories or messages interfere with reaching your dreams?
- Do you want to find ways to clear your past mistakes or failures from your mind?

The Benefits of Coming Alive to Create a Richer, Happier Life

Change is difficult only because we don't know how to create change in our lives. If any of the previous questions have crossed your mind, coming alive is your way forward.

Let's start by discussing the benefits of creating a richer, happier life when you Come Alive. Then I will answer the question, "Why Come Alive?"

When you embrace your journey to Come Alive to create a richer, happier life, you will confidently find who you are—

your authentic, true self. You will see life through the eyes of love and compassion and receive love and compassion in return. You find the foundation of that richer, happier life.

During your journey of coming alive, you might find you are as electrified and inspired as I was when I ran across a powerful quote from Howard Thurman: “Don’t ask what the world needs. Ask what makes you Come Alive and go do it. Because what the world needs is people who have Come Alive.”

Thurman’s quote was a turning point for me because my life’s purpose became clear. You, too, can experience an electrifying turning point—then another and another. This is a description of a richer, happier life.

You will also learn how any unconscious messages from your past (I call them blank spots) may be in your way of coming alive. Those will be graphically and profoundly revealed. Your openness to your process of solution-finding when you find new blank spots will become a lifetime strategy that will bring you success with every goal you set. You will find you live in a whole new paradigm.

The most valuable benefit is seeing how your life experiences—both good experiences and difficult ones—are woven together to keep you leveling up to new awareness, wisdom, and life skills, forming an entirely new definition of what a richer, happier life can be.

Here's what coming ALIVE means:

Coming alive is a process you learn to find the life skills to live your authentic self, know you are worthy of success, love, and fun, and, especially, find your true voice. Here's an example of a coming alive process you might consider.

A - Acknowledge your issue or problem and **ask** for what you want.

If you aren't reaching every goal you set, would you like to know why?

Would you like to know how to ask for everything you want?

L - Launch your inner detective to research information needed for change.

What resources can you use to search for the new information you need to move toward your goal?

If you knew your challenges contained the information needed to reach your goals, would you view those challenges differently?

I - Initiate your personal solution-finding process to help you face the challenges that change can bring.

Would you like to figure out your best strategy for solving problems?

Have you found a personal solution-finding process that

works every time?

V – View your life experiences and obstacles with mental focus and emotional strength.

Are you clear what being mentally focused and emotionally strong means for you and how important those are for being successful?

Is staying focused hard for you?

Do you have emotional reactions that cause you difficulties and want to change that pattern?

E – Experience the change through knowing what to expect and how to practice making that change a part of your new life.

Why Come Alive in Creating a Richer, Happier Life?

There are many more reasons and benefits to coming alive. The way to get to your new world where the "why" answer is, is to know you are already there. It surrounds you and is deep within you. You have what it takes. You have the direction. You have the courage. Just open your heart to the fact that love is always the answer and put a large measure of love in everything you do.

To Come Alive is to take life by the tail and tossing it in any direction your heart desires. Can you imagine whatever challenge you feel is something you can physically grab and toss into the heavens? Then can you envision the heavens tossing that obstacle back, fully transformed?

NOTE: *Unconscious instead of subconscious is used in this book to mean memories, feelings, and other mental content outside conscious awareness.*

Would you like to know how to handle your new world as you succeed in the changes you make?

How would you like these words and phrases to define your life: alive, vital, fulfilled, vigorous, enthusiastic, wonderful tribe of friends, plenty of discretionary money, spiritually and politically aware, mindful, present-moment living, dream job, peace, and whatever else excites you about your life?

Therefore, in answer to the question, "Why Come Alive?" the answer is simple—you will not be satisfied until you do because the very essence of your nature is to Come Alive.

One Additional Question

One more question you may have is how is this book different from other books about personal development? There are numerous distinctive differences:

This book is different because of the concept called blank spots. This concept provides a different way to look at limiting thinking, those patterns you're aware of, and those you aren't aware of. With knowledge of which blank spots you have and how to manage them or let them go, you develop new strategies and boost your ability to work through whatever is in your way to live the life of your visions.

This book is different because there are only five concepts to grasp. Once understood and practiced, these five fundamentals allow you to jump into the kind of life flow where you create your life instead of constantly reacting to what happens. To put this another way, once you have these five skills, your life will Come Alive because you will know what to do and what to expect.

This book is different because those five skills use what you already know, and the process only requires you to comprehend these principles a little more deeply. They are: (1) learning to clarify what you want and get focused, (2) start researching the new understanding that will bring change, (3) formalize a solution-finding process, (4) learn how to use your feelings to motivate yourself, and (5) discover how to live practically in your Come Alive world.

Time to Come Alive?

When your life comes alive, your entire world will change. Your life will unfold and take up residence in a delightful place. My own new world is exciting, and far beyond my wildest dreams. Does having this same feeling appeal to you?

CHAPTER ONE

Problems and More Problems

"Are problems a stop sign, or a signal to keep moving? How you feel about problems will define how successful you are in coming alive."
CORALEE KULMAN

Acknowledgement Is the Beginning

It is human nature to seek emotional, mental, physical, and spiritual balance and to continue to grow and learn. If you focus on what people might think of you or things you don't want, you create blocks in your natural quest to seek balance and wholeness. Your awareness may be lacking. You may have put on a happy face and ignored the feelings buried deep within. A part of you, however, knows something isn't right.

Remember the Hans Christian Andersen tale of *The Emperor's New Clothes,* where two weavers promised the emperor they would make him a new suit of clothes that would be invisible to those who were stupid, incompetent, or unfit for their positions? No one dared admit they couldn't see the new clothes, even the emperor himself, until a child said, "He is wearing nothing at all."

Often, you can't see the issues you face. They may be unconscious, or you may have developed distractions to avoid thinking about them. Like the emperor in the tale, others may see what is going on, but you don't. Friends and family may be hesitant to say anything.

This chapter is about what a well-known psychologist says: "You can't change what you don't acknowledge." By the end of this chapter, you will become clear about obstacles that may be keeping you from coming alive. If you are candid and frank about what is going on in your life, you have taken the first step toward awareness and change.

How Do You Face Life's Problems?

When people facing challenges attempt to work them out, they usually fall into one of five general categories. Do you see yourself in one of the categories listed below?

Reactors Those who experience constant drama and crisis. They usually aren't skilled in dealing with their emotional reactions or finding solutions. The Reactor could be in victim mode and has not learned to be proactive. They neglect to look inside themselves for answers.

Secret Keepers Those who have a secret life based on some underlying fear or unconscious belief that others might think they are bad, weak, or stupid and won't like them if they are authentic. Their problems rarely see the light of day. A Secret Keeper's personality can be hypervigilant. They tend to watch for any signal, as slight as a raised eyebrow, that may indicate the other person disagrees with them. They don't want people to know they have secret troubles or doubts they can't solve. They can feel lonely and empty.

Blanks Those who haven't received enough information or who were misinformed in their childhood. They tend to flounder around, trying to make life less stressful.

	A Blank's underlying personality style is confusion, with possible depression. They might be dealing with addictions as well. They often feel lonely and empty, too.
Hopeful Sorts	Those who live a functional life though, at times, feel a nagging sense of emptiness. Because they are unsure about what they are feeling, they live in hope that something will finally change for them.
Solution Finders	Those who have learned fear is a signal to move forward. They work through their fear or doubt and create change. They have developed a personal solution-finding process that serves them well when they face challenges.

Whatever your underlying style, learning to become a Solution Finder gives you the ability to tackle life's challenges and helps you Come Alive. It all starts with acknowledging your troubles and investigating possible solutions until answers become clear.

What Are Problems?

The *Merriam-Webster* definition that most fits in the context of this book is, "a source of perplexity, distress, or vexation."

When you engage your inner detective as you face your life's challenges, your conclusion about problems may turn out to be that your challenges provide the answers you need to understand how to reach your goals.

Problems hold the seeds of growth and transformation if you look a little deeper. When you delve into your thoughts and feelings related to a problem, you will learn valuable information about yourself and your position on issues. You then build a repertoire of solutions or positions to live your life by.

Let's see if some inner detective work on the nature of problems helps you.

A View of Problems that Might Hold You Back

Often, problems are perceived as a sign there is something wrong with you, or you're going in the wrong direction. This outlook could slow you down considerably. It's time to examine these perceptions.

There can often be a fear that the solution to the problem might bring tremendous change. An example might be this: you find your job is boring and offers little to engage your interests. You might want to consider a new job or career path; however, this kind of huge change may feel scary.

Sometimes it feels like the problems just keep coming. If you decide to take each one on and master it, that process takes time and effort. This may feel intimidating and tiring.

A View of Problems that Brings New Information

Here are a few thoughts on this:

- Problems can help you clarify and have a deeper understanding of your concerns, so you can make better decisions. For example, something struck you as being off with what someone said to you. Their comment created a reaction. When you take the time to ask yourself what is going on, you come to realize that comment triggered the memory of something your father or mother used to say and you didn't like how it felt then and the memory of that causes the same feeling now. By identifying the fact that you're reacting in response to a past issue and not a current one, you can then move back to the present to see if you're living in the past, or if this new scenario is something you need to think about more.

- Problems can help you discover, in more depth, your love, strength, and mental clarity. An example of this might be in a disagreement with a friend or family member. This problem can, when communication between the parties is respectful and curious, help one another understand each other more.

- Problems can help you find empathy and compassion. We never know what someone is dealing with. Often, someone in trouble acts out in frustration. If we take the problem they have created as a signal, or a call for help, instead of taking it personally or becoming defensive, the problem/solution process can bring compassionate understanding.

- Problems can help to provide a means to attain new successes, find strengths, and discover a greater wisdom. This deserves repeating. Our challenges or problems contain the seeds of transformation when we see them as opportunities to learn things that may be valuable for reaching our goals.

EXERCISE #1

Part One—Open Your Eyes

This is an exercise that might be useful if you aren't sure what the real issues are in your life. Sometimes life can put so much on your plate you may not have the time or the means to sit down and zero-in on the issues that, once resolved, might make a big difference in your life and contribute to greater happiness.

Read through the following list and check "yes" or "no." Be intuitive and don't think about your answers too hard.

For a complete list of the exercises in this book, see ***Appendix A – Exercise List.***

Questions to Determine Your Current Pressing Problems

There are over forty questions on this list. These are some of the questions you want to ask yourself about the areas of your life. In ***Appendix B – More Questions*** there are over 160 additional questions if you are interested in delving deeper.

Yes ☐ No ☐ Do you believe that by looking at your problems, solutions to them can be found?

Yes ☐ No ☐ Are you having regular "aha!" moments?

Yes ☐ No ☐ Do you know what you want?

Yes ☐ No ☐ Do you have a method to find out what you need to know, or do, to make changes?

Yes ☐ No ☐ Do you have a personal solution-finding process that makes change easier?

Yes ☐ No ☐ Do you use both your analytical mind and your feelings to move you toward change?

Yes ☐ No ☐ Have you ever made a change and found you felt awkward for a while when you start to live in a new way?

Yes ☐ No ☐ Are you motivated by feelings of excitement and passion?

Yes ☐ No ☐ Do you think feelings are important for living a good life?

Yes ☐ No ☐ Are you confident that you know how to sort out your problems?

Yes ☐ No ☐ Do you have moments when a new, inspirational thought pops into your mind that answers your latest question?

Yes ☐ No ☐ Have you experienced a time that could be called a "dark night of the soul" and come out stronger and wiser?

Yes ☐ No ☐ Are you able to acknowledge your negative side's thoughts and feelings without judgment or trying to turn them into positives?

Yes ☐ No ☐ Do you see negative thoughts as signals that something needs to shift?

Yes ☐ No ☐ Are you happy with how you treat your body?

Yes ☐ No ☐ Do you know how to access the feelings hidden in your body?

Yes ☐ No ☐ Are you comfortable with your religion or spirituality?

Yes ☐ No ☐ Do you find your spirituality helps you when you feel lost or need an answer?

Yes ☐ No ☐ Are you frustrated with politics and complain because you don't know what to do?

Yes ☐ No ☐ Are politics of great interest to you and do you get involved?

Yes ☐ No ☐ Have you explored what conflict means to you?

Yes ☐ No ☐ Have you explored the benefits of conflict?

The Meaning of Love and How to Express It

Yes ☐ No ☐ Have you explored the meaning of love?

Yes ☐ No ☐ Is love the foundation of your behaviors?

Yes ☐ No ☐ Can you show respect, authenticity, and honesty to everyone?

Yes ☐ No ☐ Are you able to hear what others are trying to say so, once heard, they can be more open to make time to hear you?

Yes ☐ No ☐ Did you feel loved by your parents?

Yes ☐ No ☐ Did you feel your parents supported you enough?

Yes ☐ No ☐ Have you learned to let go of your parents' issues?

Yes ☐ No ☐ Do you understand how to stimulate your child's (or children's) curiosity?

Yes ☐ No ☐ Do you understand the benefits of boundaries to preserve a good relationship?

Yes ☐ No ☐ Do you understand boundaries are opportunities for learning about each other?

Yes ☐ No ☐ Does your marriage or partnership have equal responsibilities? (Financial, household maintenance, laundry, grocery shopping, cooking, responsibilities for children, etc.)

Yes ☐ No ☐ Are you able to resolve issues easily?

Yes ☐ No ☐ Does your relationship with yourself include love, acceptance, and forgiveness?

Yes ☐ No ☐ Do you know how to respectfully ask others for what you want or need?

Yes ☐ No ☐ Are you open to exploring unresolved issues?

Yes ☐ No ☐ Do you have a clear purpose of what gives your life meaning?

Yes ☐ No ☐ Do you know what ignites your interest and excites you?

Yes ☐ No ☐ Have you set many goals and generally succeeded?

Yes ☐ No ☐ Do you have a personal process to be successful with goal achievement?

Yes ☐ No ☐ Do you consider failing as feedback?

Yes ☐ No ☐ Do you know how to deal with failure?

Yes ☐ No ☐ Do you feel motivated to find your way to coming alive?

Assessment of this Exercise:

Start out by patting yourself on the back. Getting through these questions shows you are serious and want to make some changes in your life. Now, count your check marks.

If you have checked eight or more yes responses, you are

a superhero and can leap tall buildings in a single bound. Please give this book to an unhappy friend or relative who needs to find out how to Come Alive.

If you have checked eight or more no responses, your "Genuinely Human Certificate" is on its way. I hope this book helps you find your inner guiding light.

Should you find yourself with a mix of positive and negative answers, you may want to examine the areas you want to strengthen.

Overall, this exercise is intended to encourage you to recognize the first component of a solution-finding process, which is to acknowledge something feels wrong or off to you and you'd like to feel better.

Did the Exercise Give You Any "Aha!" Moments?

"Aha!" moments are the motivators and nourishment for living a full life. My definition of an "aha!" moment is when the mind and heart come together in harmony and increase your chances of movement and growth. It is your authentic self that gives you the "aha!" moments. These moments provide you a wealth of information you can use to identify who you are and what you want. Keep your eyes open for the "aha!" gifts.

EXERCISE #1—PART TWO

Start an "Aha!" Moments' Journal

Consider recording your "Aha!" moments. This helps to make them concrete and memorable. Write them down in a journal, on 3 x 5 cards, take notes on your phone, or type a list on your computer.

Questions for Reflection:

This finishes the exploration of problems and their acknowledgement. Here are a few additional questions to consider:

- What is your understanding about the meaning of obstacles that come up in your life?
- Do you believe those challenges are a path to new information?
- Do problems make you angry, resentful, or depressed because you don't know what to do?
- Have your problems interrupted your life?
- What feelings did this chapter bring up for you?

Summary

The reason we have explored problems in depth is because there are many myths and taboos about them. When you acknowledge problems and work on solving them, solutions begin to unfold. Remember what Deepak Chopra said: “If you live the questions, life will move you into the answers.”

My hope is by the end of this book you will see your challenges in a different and more empowering manner.

CHAPTER TWO

"What Do You Mean I Have a Problem?"

"Telling someone what they are doing is wrong or saying they have a problem will often bring defensiveness. Appreciating what they are doing right leads to openness, trust, and solutions."

CORALEE KULMAN

ME AT 315 POUNDS

"Extremely defensive" would describe my reaction to someone telling me I might have some problems. I was adept at ignoring the reality of one big problem—that I was 5'2"and weighed 315 pounds at the time of this picture. It really didn't register. To others, my problems were obvious. Morbid obesity is what my doctor's chart said. Walking twenty feet would cause my legs and back to hurt and I'd be out of breath. Evidence piled up when buying size 4x clothing and using an extension seat belt to fly on an airplane. Still, my mind and heart avoided the reality of my situation.

Relationships, work, family life, even personal interests didn't give me even a small measure of peace or joy. A sense of emptiness and unhappiness were my constant companions. Looking back now, I see my life was a desperate, urgent search for peace and fulfillment. The questions I asked you to consider in the previous chapter were essentially an inventory of the issues I faced.

My desire to find peace of mind and connection to others kept tugging at my heart. What made being in touch with reality illusive for me, and could also be true for you, is many of my issues were buried deep in my unconscious mind. I didn't know how to access what was real, and I also lacked information to help me clarify my situation. These unseen issues are what I now call "blank spots." When my path led me to learn how to discover and explore those blank spots, life started to change.

A blank spot is a concept I use to describe the inability to see one's ineffective or destructive thought patterns and behaviors. A blank spot is partly a loss of the ability to access true feelings. A blank spot is also an indicator that basic solution-finding skills are missing.

Blank spots are memories that have been repressed. They cause a feeling of emptiness in your being. Much is misunderstood about this emptiness.

You might think of a blank spot this way: most people grow up, finish school or college, go to work, and engage in life with a toolbox of life skills. When you have blank spots, your toolbox is missing some critical skills.

Here is another description to explain blanks spots: You may come out of childhood with a lack of understanding or with misunderstandings. Some of this could come from inexperience, while some of your ways of thinking might be caused from dysfunction in the family or from abuse. When you go out on your own and encounter problems without a basic skill set, this can often create more misunderstanding. Unconscious blank spots might be holding you back from success. Your task is to root out the blank spots and learn to manage them.

Yet another way to understand the concept of blank spots is that they are a way to explain your misunderstandings or lack of understanding. It is more useful than labeling our behaviors as character defects, which gives us little help in working through the issues in front of us."

When you Come Alive, you realize you have the power to turn your life around. You begin to recognize what you didn't comprehend before. You start to acknowledge your ability to choose new thoughts, feelings and behaviors. You master the components of coming alive: emotional strength, mental focus, physical well-being, spiritual living, political awareness, relationship skills, and manifesting. You know your authentic self and become able to see, hear, feel, and speak clearly. You find the true you.

A Deeper Look at Blank Spots

Most of us come into adulthood with some blank spots. The

inability to be clear with your thoughts and feelings comes partially from inexperience. As you develop solution-finding skills with the support of family, friends, or professional help, you grow and find the wisdom to live well. Hopefully, you manage to mature without too much crisis or too many life-altering mistakes.

The inability to see your thought and feeling patterns, or to develop solution-finding skills, often comes from growing up in a dysfunctional or abusive family. However, blank spots can also develop in healthy families because blank spots are a coping mechanism of the unconscious mind.

When you grow up in a family where conflict, misbehavior, neglect, or even abuse is present, you are too young to have concepts or language to process your experiences. Your feelings get buried in your unconscious because it is the job of the unconscious mind to prevent you from experiencing too much trauma. In response, you develop reactive, adapting behaviors and enter adulthood with "baggage."

Even when you live in a generally healthy family, the day-to-day stress of life's challenges and how family members react, vent, or even bury stress within themselves, can traumatize children without them even realizing it. Those coping mechanisms are baggage as well. Yes, blank spots are an equal-opportunity baggage maker.

Between inexperience and baggage, you step into the adult world somewhat impaired and uninformed. Life starts to become more complicated because the adaptive behavior patterns to survive or manage your childhood experiences are sometimes offensive to others. Feelings of confusion, hurt, emptiness, and the feeling of being lost may surface. You might even develop additional ineffective or destructive behaviors in reaction.

How to Recognize Blank Spots

Chances are strong that you see blank spots in others and don't see them in yourself. Here are a few indicators of people with a blank spot.

- Minor incidents cause them to have intense reactions that appear unrelated to a current event.
- People with blank spots aren't clear what triggers their anger or frustration. They may minimize the reaction, saying, or even believing, they are just in a bad mood.
- Their blank spots slip out as white lies or subtle shifts in position at the slightest indication that they might not look smart or strong.
- Their life story is hard to believe. You might call them cons or sweet-talkers.
- They are chameleon-like and agree with everything you say.
- They avoid confrontation or run from conflict at all costs.

- They complain bitterly and obsessively about how others treat them without considering how their own dysfunctional patterns contribute to the situation.
- They shut down, isolate, run away, or disappear emotionally, if not literally.
- They can't control addictions and obsessive behaviors. The heartbreak of blank spots is how blank spots affect you and those around you.

If you are curious about your potential blank spots, here are a few more ways they may present themselves:

- You react to something someone said or did so much that your reaction may startle you.
- You often feel you aren't being heard.
- You have pet peeves that cause strong reactions.
- You need to control or have a say in everything around you.
- Attempts at a positive outlook fall apart when you are stressed.
- You experience repeated failures and disappointments.
- You have conflicts with others that don't get resolved.

- You experience silence or cold shoulders from others.
- You have a constant nagging emptiness.

All of this is sad, because people are mostly good-hearted. When your blank spots show up in your actions and behaviors, you may be labeled as toxic or as having character defects. The typical reaction of others is to avoid you. If you learn to understand the missing or misunderstood information, your life will be profoundly different.

The High Inner Price of Blank Spots

The lack of awareness about patterns of behavior has a high price. People spend their entire lives stuck in a rut of circular conflicts, many with lots of drama or chaos. They may seek comfort through alcohol, drugs, food, overworking, and other distractions. Unresolved issues repeat themselves with different people and different situations. Blank spots could well be the root cause.

Do Blank Spots Help Us?

Let's step back a moment and note a comment from a therapist of mine. She suggested my way of adapting to my childhood experiences through distractions, rarely stopping, and an eating disorder, could have been the best way to manage my anxiety and pain under the circumstances. She suggested I could have gone catatonic. In other words, there were many other adaptive behaviors that could have been even more destructive.

The mind does more than help you analyze, organize, and strategize. Part of the mind's job is to protect you. When you experience trauma, abuse, a lack of nurturing, or emotional abandonment, you could experience deep disabling pain. The mind, instead, goes into a type of forgetting. This is how people survive. The mind keeps you safe, in whatever way it can, from your traumas.

Even though the mind's job is to protect you from trauma, the mind is there to help you heal, too. Thoughts and feelings, if buried, affect you for the rest of your life. Your unconscious mind will bring those forgotten experiences back to you to acknowledge and work through when you are ready. They show up as reactions, emotional charges, and flashbacks. They are signals that a part of you is out of balance. They come when you are strong enough to address them. Working through them allows you to Come Alive and create freedom and joy in your life.

What Would Life Be Like Without Blank Spots?

ME AT 100 POUNDS LESS

The adventure of growing and healing will become a way of

life for you. Rich new insights bring greater awareness. Each time this happens, a blank spot is revealed, processed, let go, replaced with new thoughts and then made practical. The concept of blank spots can open new doors to show you a way out of any chaos in your life.

Each morning will find you are enthusiastic about your life and work. You will be able to feel your feelings and understand that you don't have to act on them, just consider them. Whether those feelings are positive or appear to be negative, you will be able to acknowledge and accept them as signals to explore your thinking. Your thinking will be clearer and lovingly directed. Your mental focus will be sharp. Your spirituality, and connection to God or your Higher Power, will truly work for you, guiding you when there is a need for more information. Your political leanings will become clear and open. Relationship connections will grow and deepen. Your circle of friends will teem with caring, empowered people. You will manifest almost every goal. Even apparent obstacles will bring you enthusiasm because you now know them to be a gift of transformational information.

The inner fighting that may have plagued you in the past will be gone. You will feel at home in your own skin. There will be an underlying sense of peace and happiness that permeates your life. You will have the strength to speak your truth. This is what coming alive can look like for you.

What more could coming alive mean for you? Here are some

possibilities to consider:

- It could mean growth and uplifting insights become part of your life experience.
- It could mean you are able to respectfully express your wants and needs and have others hear you.
- It could cause you to take up a hobby, develop a new skill, or pursue a new interest.
- It could mean you feel better prepared to find a new job you love instead of only working for the money.
- It could mean all your friends become the type who celebrate you and are your cheerleaders.
- It could mean you succeed at most, if not all, of your goals.
- It could mean your marriage or partnership adds value to your life in numerous ways.
- It could mean that you take charge of your physical well-being.
- It could mean that you challenge yourself to a higher standard of living in many aspects of your life.

EXERCISE #2

Start to Explore Your Blank Spots

This exercise helps you explore the blank spots you might have.

On a piece of paper, make three columns. Label them "NAME", "WHAT BOTHERS ME", and "WHAT I APPRECIATE."

Now make a list of everyone you know under "NAME" who may cause you to have reactions to what they say or do. In the second column, "WHAT BOTHERS ME", write down those things you see in them that trouble you, focusing on the behaviors that bug you or cause you to have a reaction when you're around that person. The next step is the third column, "WHAT I APPRECIATE." In this column, write down the qualities you admire and appreciate in these people. Also, add names of other people who have qualities you appreciate if they aren't already on your list.

Now, sit down, take a deep breath and take another look. The list of bothersome things may include some of your blank spots. This is because what those people do or say wouldn't bother you if you have mastered those areas within yourself. You might even find some compassion because you understand what is causing them to behave the way they do.

Take another deep breath and look at the third column. This column has those admirable character qualities you are working on or possess yourself. You wouldn't see these qualities in others if you weren't aware of them in yourself.

Take a few moments to reflect on this exercise. See if this exercise has given you a roadmap to areas you might want to explore.

Questions for Reflection:

- Are you clear about the concept of blank spots?
- Did the concept and explanation of blank spots give you some insight into how your past may be influencing your present?
- Do you notice a lot of blank spots in others?
- Did the exercise give you any "aha!" moments about blank spots you will consider investigating?
- Do you live in reaction to life's circumstances or do you work to create a life you love?
- Are you a persistent person, or do you give up easily?
- What feelings came up for you in this chapter?

Summary

When you take the time to learn about your inner and outer life, the rewards can be profound. So many people live lives that aren't necessarily unhappy, yet they aren't joyful, either. Please take some time now to reflect on your life and your deep desires.

CHAPTER THREE

The Path to Change

"The greatest triumph in coming alive is discovering that life is always presenting you with opportunities to make changes that will level-up your awareness and life skills. When you learn your personal process for making changes, they then come easier and quicker."

CORALEE KULMAN

Life has a way of pressing you toward change. Occasionally, you aim for it and at other times change comes flying at you. The complexity of change and the discomfort it can cause may confuse you at times.

Those discomforts can shake your emotional, mental, physical, spiritual, financial, and relationship worlds. However, as each one of those discomforts comes up, it helps to know these are opportunities to grow and understand so much more about yourself. Change can turn into a welcome friend, representing hope, if you learn how useful change can be.

Resistance to Change

There are people who strongly resist change. While a part of me craved getting unstuck, another part of me vigorously resisted change. The skills for me to create change didn't exist, in part because of a closed mind and many fears. A friend of mine said change felt like terror to her.

However, when you think about it, each day you are challenged by change. The weather changes. Your finances change. Jobs come and go. Your moods change. Things wear out and must be replaced in your home and car. Your body can be injured or become sick and require healing attention. Conflicts come up. Friends and family move out of your life or pass on. Your children grow up. You age.

You manage changes in your life all the time, even if you don't think you do. If you find you have resistance to change, this could be a blank spot. This is the time to launch your inner detective to see what is underneath your resistance to change. What follows may help.

The Most Common Change Blank Spot

There are many stumbling blocks—blank spots—that get in the way of creating the kind of changes in your life that help you Come Alive. Let me explain one blank spot that gets in the way of change by sharing a personal experience.

While making progress in healing an eating disorder, the emotional triggers to my food bingeing started to come to light. Those triggers ran the gamut—emotional, physical, spiritual, and many, many mental triggers, too. For example, being extremely tired was a trigger that would lead to overeating.

When I understood what those triggers looked and felt like, they could no longer sneak up, catch me off guard, and lead to unconsciously seeking food to numb them. Instead, awareness of those triggers prepared me and helped me become emotionally strong. This made making different and better choices easier. With ease came more change.

The same holds true for everyone who wants to make changes or reach goals. If you are aware of your personal stumbling blocks or triggers and how they look and feel, you will have a better success rate.

Before we explore the details of how to make changes, here's how some of your struggles might be different from those of others. When you look for a process for change, knowing what "level" of difficulty you face may facilitate movement and growth.

Life's Challenges

Life's challenges are different for everyone. Abraham Maslow in his Hierarchy of Needs Theory offers some clarity about how different your life can be from others. Maslow describes two levels of life challenges. One is your safety and security. The other is your esteem and self-actualization.

In other words, you may struggle to put food on the table and pay your bills because of financial or debt-related issues. You may have a difficult marriage, trouble with work, or conflicted relationships. These issues would be at the "survival" or "existence" level and reside in the area of safety and security.

Then there are those who have found some stability with their finances and relationships, yet they still feel empty and unfulfilled. That is another level which is related to coming alive or self-actualizing. This would be in the esteem and self-actualization level.

The difference in the two levels of challenges is the survival level could mean physical or emotional existence. Survival is a clear necessity. The Come-Alive level is a more of a deep *wanting*. The point in this is that you can change your life no matter where you are in the hierarchy of needs. Once you have mastered how change works, you can use the process to fulfill any goal or intention your heart desires. If you feel you have too much to change, consider the following chapters on change and experiment with the process to see if you can simplify it for yourself. The process works with any of life's challenges.

The Path to Coming Alive

The following chapters are a step-by-step description on how to make change. Each one of them in itself can bring change. Each chapter will describe the step, what to expect, and the blank spots that might be getting in the way of your success.

The most important realization that may come during the process of learning about change could be put into these words: the effort you put into making changes takes no more effort, maybe even less, than the effort and energy needed to deal with the frustration and failure, as well as having to mend the ramifications of being stuck in misguided behaviors. This observation can turn into a guiding principle and make future changes more attractive. Give some thought to this possibility.

EXERCISE #3

Change is Letting Go and Finding a Replacement

This exercise is to support you in understanding change better. One important aspect of change is realizing whatever you want to change needs to be replaced with something just as emotionally helpful for the change to be permanently successful. For example, you decide to eat a healthier diet. However, certain foods may have emotional connections for you—comfort, companionship, soothing emotions, and many other possibilities. When you change your diet, if you don't find other ways to fill those needs, you might be headed for failure.

When the concept that food was a comforter and a soother became clear to me, I found a book by Susan Albers, Psy.D. called *50 Ways to Soothe Yourself without Food*. This book helped pave the way in my journey out of emotional eating because there were many interesting ways to soothe myself. Just opening the book often changed my mood.

Here is how you can put this concept to work. Decide on

something you want to change. Choose anything that seems to bother you a great deal.

Take some time and journal or reflect on what you may be getting from your current situation. Maybe food is a comfort. Maybe venting is your method to release frustrations. The problem may come when your venting upsets those around you. The idea is to focus on what you might do to replace behaviors you want to change. Maybe doing some stress releasing exercises such as ones you can find on YouTube about bioenergetics or trauma release will help. Maybe a walk will allow you time to figure out a measured response—if you even need to respond.

When you see those areas you want to change, remember they need to be replaced by something that satisfies you.

Questions for Reflection:

- Have you accepted that the bumps in the road you call life are permanent, or do you think change is possible?
- Have you looked your problems squarely in the eye and welcomed them for what they are: messages containing the seeds of transformation?
- Are you serious and persistent, even in the face of obstacles?
- Do you challenge any thoughts that slow or block

your way to success?

- Have you made "friends" with change?
- What did you feel after you read this chapter?

Summary

Embracing change can be like walking with a friend beside you. If you want the confidence to say you reach every goal you set and find harmony in your emotional, mental, physical, spiritual, political, and relationship worlds, know that change is the vehicle to get there.

Here is some encouraging advice to end this chapter:

> *"The only way to make sense out of change is to plunge into it, move with it, and join the dance."*
> ALAN WATTS

CHAPTER FOUR

Step One—Acknowledge and Ask

"If you don't know what you want, and you keep failing to achieve anything, you have just proven the principle of 'what you focus on increases'."

CORALEE KULMAN

Acknowledge Your Issue or Goal and Ask for What You Want

In the previous chapters, we explored the importance of identifying problems or issues as the vital first step to help you define your goals and the changes you desire. We also explored how you may struggle with unconscious blank spots that make identification of personal issues difficult.

Even if you have some problems you can't readily identify, you will still be able to move forward. You start by asking for what you want. The unconscious blank spots will reveal themselves in the process of working toward a goal. They show up in your emotions as doubts, worries, or fears. They could also come in the form of "aha!" moments. In other words, anything that is out of the ordinary is a signal.

What to Expect

When you start to dream and visualize in wonderful detail what you want, change starts, and goals begin to manifest. During this process, focus specifically on what you want and let go of what you don't want. When you do, momentum builds. The key motivation must be from the passion in your heart. With that passion, you sustain your momentum when challenges, even obstacles, come up. This can't be emphasized enough.

What does it mean when it's said that the key motivation must be from the passion in your heart? Here's a scenario to describe it: You embark on a new goal to create a change in your life. You might be excited, hopeful, and enthusiastic. You clearly know what you want. Motivation oozes from your every thought and feeling.

Then the obstacles come. That's okay, because you know

digging deeper for the transformational information in those obstacles is a part of the solution-finding process. At this point, your experiences might start to feel like a tense inner challenge. Vulnerability and doubt could radiate from other parts of your life as well. With a passion for your goal, you can find the understanding that will lead you to transformation insights. One way to look at this blank spot is to say you have fallen apart and now you are ready to put the pieces together in the way you want.

You can recognize you have a blank spot when you see yourself flailing around in confusion. You may feel off balance, even disoriented. These feelings are signals that your mind is bringing up unconscious blank spots for you to process and understand so you can move toward the changes you want. This is, in part, the answer you are looking for. Engage your passion and desire to help yourself be persistent about reaching your goal and seeking the new understanding that will help move you toward success. Knowing this can help keep you motivated when your scattered mind tempts you to get lost in fear and doubt. Viewing this time as a celebration, too, will help lead to your success.

Acknowledge, Then Ask—The Blank Spots

On the surface, focusing on what you want seems obvious. However, you might be surprised by how many people focus on what they *don't* want. They are a bit surprised when they are guided, instead, to work to articulate, visualize, and feel what their ideal would be if things changed.

WHAT YOU FOCUS ON INCREASES

This concept isn't some airy-fairy, woo-woo stuff. It is simple logic. If you don't know what you want, you will stay stuck and destined to live a circular life, returning to where you are, time after time.

When you focus on what you want, that process gets every part of your mind zeroing in on ways to support you. In this way, the entire universe supports you—it's one of those universal laws.

It is often a bit of a challenge to avoid getting lost in all the problems that come up when you pursue a goal or want to make a change in your life. However, the willingness to be persistent about keeping the result in mind is a sure way to help yourself manifest what you desire.

If you aren't sure how this works, try it, test it, see it as an experiment.

YOU ARE ONLY ABLE TO CHANGE YOURSELF

People who want coaching often come with relationship struggles. Generally, they have spent many hours attempting to change the mind of the other person. They believe once the other person understands their point of view, their relationship will smooth out. Getting other people to change rarely works because people will vehemently resist another person telling them how they need to be different. People tend to get defensive when they are being told they are wrong.

Here's what works. When you start to make changes in your own outlook and behaviors, those changes affect those around you and almost always affect them in a positive way.

When you are more confident, authentic, and speak your truth respectfully, your openness encourages others to do the same. Your behavior might even become a model. Movement often follows.

CHANGE IS ABOUT UNDERSTANDING

Change requires new understanding. If you understood how to reach your goal or make the change you want, you would have done it already. Right? When you keep hoping that doing the same things you are doing will just make it happen, you have a blank spot.

People who are successful are always on a new learning path. They have developed the confidence that they can learn what they need to do to move forward. This process is similar to developing a new skill, such as painting. You learn about canvases, paints, technique, etc. It's no different when learning life skills. You learn to watch for processes and patterns and how you can incorporate them into your life.

When you take the attitude that a successful life is about learning and understanding, you've mastered this blank spot . . . or any blank spot for that matter.

EXERCISE #4

What Do You Want?

This exercise is an opportunity to get clear on what you want. Pick out an area in your life you are struggling with. Start with a small goal. Begin to visualize in detail what you want. Put strong emotions behind this visualization. Feel your desire for this goal well up in every part of your mind, heart, and body.

Record your journey so you learn how your process works as you move toward your goal. Once you've succeeded, reflect on that writing. Did you have a dream or vision? Did some new, unexpected idea pop into your mind to guide you to do something? Did you journal about your goal and find something that then became clear?

Questions for Reflection

- What does "digging deeper" mean to you?
- Have you been able to switch your focus from what you don't want towards being more specific with what you do want?

- Have you been frustrated because your goals involve having someone else change?
- Are you ready to start by changing yourself first?
- Do you see the logic that reaching a new goal is about reaching a new understanding?
- How did this chapter feel to you?

Summary

Defining the problems or issues in your life is the foundation for being able to bring about change. Knowing what you specifically want, in major detail—thoughts and feelings, accompanied by visions—provides the ingredients that pull all your inner and outer resources together to create what you are looking for. Your mind begins to cooperate, unfolding ideas and directions in which to go. Your heart begins to motivate you to keep going when challenges appear.

CHAPTER FIVE

Step Two—
Launch Your Inner Detective

"Your lack of understanding yourself gets in your way more than anything else when you're working towards achieving your goals."

CORALEE KULMAN

Launch Your Inner Detective

Any goal or change in your life will require information you don't presently have. Logically, you would have reached your goal or made changes if you knew what to do and how to get there. If you believe otherwise, you might want to consider that you have a blank spot. It is like that saying attributed to Albert Einstein about doing the same thing over and over again and expecting different results. It's time for a new perspective or strategy.

You may experience your inner detective as curiosity or critical thinking. Whatever you call your inner detective, using that mental tool is the way you begin to learn and sort out what you don't understand. Usually, you will be led to an "aha!" moment that will show up as new thoughts that jump up out of nowhere. You might read an article or book, or see a movie, then a new thought inspires you. Maybe someone you talk to has a turn of a phrase that changes your perspective. Perhaps you attend a class or workshop and the teacher describes a new and wonderful process that resonates.

In those moments, your heart might burst with joy because you see what has held you back. At other times, you find hope simply because you realize you're experiencing growth and movement at last. You might see the experience as a missing piece of who you are that has come forward. When you experience the results of your inner detective's work and experience the rewards of obtaining new information, you may be hooked!

Launching your inner detective leads you to fill your mind with as much information as possible on whatever subject you are stuck on. This activity is a signal to the unconscious that you are serious about wanting to move to the next step in your growth, or that you're ready to reach a goal.

The one concept to keep in mind is when you have launched your inner detective, you aren't looking for detailed "how-to's", you are only looking for the next step. This new step-by-step information will bring an unfolding of what you need to know to grow and move on. Look for the information to pop out in any "aha!" form.

If you love a good mystery and figure most mysteries out before the truth is revealed, you might find this concept captures your interest. When you visualize launching your inner detective, see yourself as shining a flashlight into your inner world.

What to Expect

Change could shake your world as you know it. New information might surprise or even shock you. When you expect this, you're prepared, and navigating is easier. Remember, you want change because you are uncomfortable in the life you are currently living.

This vulnerable time is the time when change happens because your inner detective hits the "aha!" information you just found. These are the exact moments when you ask yourself if you are wholeheartedly and deeply serious about making change.

When you expect and know it is all right to be vulnerable

and overwhelmed, even fearful, you can feel some patience with the process. Feel those feelings without judgment. These are honest feelings and are crucial, even cathartic, in the process of change. Embrace them. Radically accept them by not judging them.

When the going gets tough, it's almost over. Victory is near.

Launch Your Inner Detective—The Blank Spots

What you don't understand, or what is buried in your past's unconscious misunderstandings, might disrupt your journey. Setting your intention to launch your inner detective brings the inner detective right out to find what blank spots are in the way.

OBSTACLES AND CHALLENGES CONTAIN TRANSFORMATIONAL INFORMATION

Another life-altering time for me came while attending the June 24, 2012 sermon by Dr. Michael Beckwith of *The Secret* fame at Agape International Spiritual Center in Culver City, California. His sermon was titled *No Labels, No Limitations.* Dr. Beckwith's words related to obstacles containing transformational information. That got my attention. He said that if you didn't label obstacles as good or bad, but were open to their lessons, you could be transformed. A major epiphany came with this vital, useful information. My view of life's challenges changed. I reframed my thinking and started to focus on what I was learning and life took off in great new directions.

If you view life's challenges and obstacles in this way, you will start to welcome them. What a concept!

NOTE: *Dr. Beckwith's sermon can be found in the Agape International website in the streaming archives for 6/24/12 11 a.m. service.*

UNCONSCIOUS MADE CONSCIOUS

There are many methods of accessing what you are unaware of in your unconscious. Neuro-linguistic programming, hypnosis, journaling, meditation, and just plain asking are a few methods. A simple method is asking, "What is it I need to understand to ______________________?"

The reason this endeavor is important is because blank spots—those misunderstandings that are rolling around in your unconscious—get in the way of success. When you start a process by setting an intention, goal, or want to make a change, the thoughts and feelings that come up—both negative and positive—are your mind signaling you that you may need to learn more by digging deeper. You have made the unconscious conscious when you look at those signals and have mastered this blank spot.

EVERYTHING MATTERS

Have you become weary from the constant barrage of problems in your life? Are you someone who is looking for the one insight that will solve everything? Despite the disappointment of not finding that miraculous insight, everything you have learned will end up becoming useful.

Coaches may discuss your past experiences to help you know you are understood but, more importantly, this allows them to find a way to reframe experiences that will help you move out of what has kept you stuck. This will help you let go of not seeing how important everything that has happened to you truly is.

If you step back a bit and look at your life and how it has unfolded, you will see your experiences aren't always random. Instead, they eventually weave together a scenario that leads to your growth and success. They will give you a huge clue to your life's purpose as well.

The willingness to keep looking for what you need to understand will put pieces of information, called wisdom, into your identity structure.

EXERCISE #5

Launch Your Inner Detective

Ask yourself, "What is the most pressing problem I face?" Start your detective work. Go to Amazon and find a book. Google the issue. Search Google Scholar and you'll have access to scholarly papers, academic articles, as well as case law. Check out documentaries, videos, or audio books. Go to the library and check out their reference materials.

You'll also want to talk to others. Hearing another person's perspective may incite fresh ways of thinking and provide "aha!" moments.

Note your process and what it reveals for you.

Questions for Reflection

- What form does your inner detective take? Is your detective a researcher? Is it filled with curiosity?
- How do you feel about the idea of launching your inner detective?

- Have you used your inner detective all along and didn't realize that is what you do?
- Are you open to seeing the challenges that come into your life as containing transformation information?
- Do you know the unconscious and conscious mind are always working to support you?
- Does reflecting on what you have learned when you've gone down a path that didn't work out help you move forward?
- How did you feel about this chapter?

Summary

Your inner detective is at work, even if you don't know it. Your mind is always working to bring harmony and wholeness to your life. The goal is to learn to consciously direct your inner detective to learn what you are interested in. When you are stumped or hit a roadblock, having a process or a question to ask yourself opens the resources of your mind. There are answers and guidance for every challenge you have if you put your inner detective to work.

CHAPTER SIX

Step Three—
Initiate Your Personal Solution-Finding Process

"When you take one step toward solving a problem, you have stepped out of the problem and into the solution. This puts you in a whole different energy."

CORALEE KULMAN

A Formal Solution-Finding Process

How do you step into solving a problem? One way is to have a personal solution-finding process you call on whenever an issue comes up that requires more than a simple decision.

When asked, most people concede they haven't considered a personal solution-finding method. Mostly, people just react and wing it through their troubles, relying on past experiences that may or may not have worked.

If you have a method of finding solutions, life's challenges will be less likely to throw you. Obstacles get resolved because you now have a tool. Even vulnerability from having the difficulty becomes manageable.

The idea of a personal process came to me during a difficult time with a friend. Something led me to try a different approach instead of going into my usual overreacting or fix-it mode. Those modes rarely worked anyway. What did I try? Patience. I thought maybe sitting for a while and giving myself some time to reflect on what had happened might bring a different result.

In that time of reflection, a profound insight came: my initial reactions were from old messages from the past. Those reactions didn't contain useful information or solutions for my current troubles. They didn't address the real issue. When stepping back, however, useful information and solutions about the real issue did start to come, and I was able to work things out with that friend.

This experience made me curious. Could this delaying technique become a process to use whenever a challenge presented itself? Maybe this could be a method to use to find solutions for many of my struggles.

What evolved turned into a personal solution-finding method that I've used to create some powerful changes. That process turned out to be much better than expected. It is a method you, too, can use to find solutions.

When you are interested in changing your financial or material prosperity, personality traits or habits, addictions, marriage, relationships, communication skills, health or weight, or any aspect of your life, everything is generally achieved through a process. Rarely is there an "aha!" moment that suddenly changes everything.

Here is a potential process to use. You can always create your own, too.

- First, identify the difficulty. Give the issue a name, label, or identity.
- Acknowledge that your initial reaction is probably caused by old programming or habits. (This can bring enough understanding that you'll be able to move on to finding the real issue.)
- Calmly reflect on what happened, or talk to a trusted friend. What are the feelings underneath your reaction?
- Ask for guidance. Your resource might be God, your Higher Power, Universal Wisdom, the

Universe—whatever works best for you.

- The next step is to practice patience while waiting for guidance. If patience feels difficult, journal your thoughts and feelings to help you let go of the noise in your head. Another way to help you be patient is to organize something in your home that has been bothering you. Sometimes making your environment orderly helps your thoughts become orderly.
- Act on the guidance.
- Express gratitude.

Shape your personal steps around your belief system or lifestyle. The whole point is to find a conscious method to use anytime you have difficulty. You might also try spontaneous sketching, mind-mapping, or any other method that helps you find solutions to your troubles. As you customize your process to fit your own interests, lifestyle, and beliefs, use the criteria your process provides to attain a higher level of success.

What to Expect

Start the solution-finding process by identifying the issue, setting an intention or goal, and launching your inner detective. You might start to hit obstacles, whether they are self-doubts or negativity that comes up for you, or challenges in relationships, work, or other aspects of your life. In fact, it is probably wise to expect something to come up. At this point you could find you feel vulnerable or confused. This may well be the beginning of the change you seek.

This confusion or vulnerability is what you want, because this is your unconscious mind re-evaluating and bringing up memories or beliefs to support your goal and, more importantly, trying to help you discover the blank spots getting in your way.

Neuro-linguistic programming teacher, Dr. Matthew James of The Empowerment Partnership, puts it this way: your conscious mind is the captain and your unconscious is the crew. When you "instruct" your crew to make a change, or manifest a goal, your unconscious goes to work.

In other words, you can expect even your own mind to create some signals for you to explore and to solve. Keep searching and searching. At some point, the pieces will come together and provide the insight you're looking for.

Initiate Your Personal Solution-Finding Process—The Blank Spots

In early adulthood, my greatest limiting belief centered around thinking something was seriously wrong because I was experiencing so many problems and crises which made my life feel chaotic. Yes, something was wrong, but my thinking something was wrong with me wasn't the problem. The "wrong" centered around thinking problems defined me.

My view of life came from an illusion that everyone else lived a problem-free life. I chuckle these days when I remember that belief. Eventually, it became clear that life always has struggles and challenges for everyone and, maybe, learning to manage these might be the direction to go.

Then, for years, my focus turned into being a champion of developing solution-finding skills. There is a flaw in this thinking, too. If you are looking to be a solution-finder, you will keep getting more problems to solve; remember that thought "what you focus on increases?" However, if you take a fresh view about what problems truly are—containing seeds of transformational information—you will start to make some movement and progress. The following blank spots will open your eyes to conflicts/obstacles/challenges and give you a whole new context from which to view your circumstances. Challenges may even be welcomed.

EMPOWERMENT THROUGH RADICAL ACCEPTANCE

Radical acceptance is a powerful concept, a life-changing concept. Radical acceptance allows you to step back, stop the inner fighting, and explore the real you. When you stop fighting what you think are negative emotions, you essentially take your power back.

You start to accept every part of you—the whole person—positive, negative, and neutral. That acceptance frees you and allows you to see yourself as empowered! Doubt and confusion leave. Others can no longer cause you to experience an emotional charge or reaction. When you add a solution-finding process with radical acceptance, you have taken growth and progress by the tail. You have started to empower yourself in this acceptance and move into more balance and wholeness—the beginning of learning to become truly authentic.

If you need more information about radical acceptance, I'd suggest reading Dr. Tara Brach's book, *Radical Acceptance: Embracing Your Life with the Heart of a Buddha.* Dr. Brach teaches you how to feel your feelings without judgment or the need to reject them.

BE TRUE TO YOURSELF

You may wonder why being true to yourself, being authentic, is in this "finding solutions" chapter. The answer is simple: you may be your own greatest obstacle. You may have unclear thinking, an inability to recognize your blank spots, lack of knowledge about the process of change, or lack solution-finding skills. Your difficulties are rarely anything outside yourself, because in the bigger picture of life you may not have control of anything that happens. However, you do have control over how you react and manage outside events. Therefore, finding solutions begins and ends with the inner you.

The best way to decide if you're being true to yourself is by watching to see if you have times you feel hesitant or disagree with someone and then find a way to express your views authentically and respectfully. When this happens, you will have experienced being true to yourself.

Being respectfully authentic will, nine times out of ten, and maybe ten times out of ten, be one of the best solution-finding approaches you can use. When you participate in humanities' inauthentic dance, meaning you attempt in a misguided way to connect with others or solve problems at the level you perceive they might want them to be addressed, you might create more problems down the road.

Taking the courage to be authentic, however, will allow you to be open in your relationships and give you the grace to face life's challenges head-on and let go of anything less. Why? Because you have come to trust your process with anything you experience.

FEEDBACK SPEEDS YOUR GROWTH

Are you hesitant or sensitive about hearing what others think about you or about a situation you were involved in? When you become open to feedback from others as part of your solution-finding process, your growth will accelerate. This willingness means you have recognized you don't know everything, and you have opened your mind and heart to new perspectives. Otherwise, you may be making the mistake of thinking that feedback from others means you are stupid or can't figure things out yourself. That attitude will often derail you, and it is NOT true. No one knows everything.

Becoming open to feedback will provide a life-shifting

awareness, another "aha!" moment. Feedback can come in many forms.

- You may get the same message from several different sources.
- When talking with trusted friends or family, you may learn that different perspectives provide wonderful feedback.
- Failure is feedback. Failure teaches you what doesn't work. Failure can be valuable.
- Someone's reaction to what you have said is feedback. Learning to acknowledge another person's reaction, even their subtle facial or body changes, can open the door to a more effective discussion. Reactions from others may tell you if your communication is effective, too.
- Someone's lack of reaction to what you have said is also feedback. There are times when people decide they are too vulnerable, or the situation is too complex for them to address what you said right away. This can be the most difficult kind of feedback because it feels personal. This hesitancy may be related to their own blank spots.
- Paraphrasing is an excellent form of feedback that is useful in conflict communication. When you learn to paraphrase by giving feedback on

what you have heard, several things happen. The other person may see they need to clarify what they meant in more depth. Occasionally, a person will realize what they are saying makes no sense or is creating an unnecessary conflict. With this recognition, they will sometimes change their position.

EXERCISE #6

Create Your Personal Solution-Finding Process

This exercise is to help you find your special solution-finding method. Start with looking for what works for you, whether it's journaling, spontaneous sketching, mind-mapping, or some other form of discovery. If you are inspired to do so, do some research on Google or in the library and find a book that inspires you.

Once you have found your process, make sure you test it to see if you have found the process that is successful on an ongoing basis.

Questions for Reflection

- Do you already have a personal solution-finding process? What is it?
- Have you practiced radical acceptance to reduce your inner fighting?
- What reaction did you have when you read the statement "being true to yourself is a good way to

find solutions?"

- Are you open to feedback? Why or why not?
- How did this chapter feel to you?

Summary

When you focus on meeting challenges head-on, with the understanding they contain important information in your journey to Come Alive, you soon master solution-finding and may even welcome challenges.

Once you have developed your own solution-finding process and you begin to sort out the dilemmas that your find yourself in, you will move out of the difficulties enlightened and filled with the joy of success.

CHAPTER SEVEN

Step Four— View Life with Mental Focus and Emotional Strength

> *"All growth requires mental focus and emotional strength. Otherwise, you are blown around randomly and your choices become limited."*
>
> CORALEE KULMAN

As you deal with the obstacles your new goals may bring, your focus can dim and emotions can cause you to weaken your resolve. This could cause your path to feel bumpy, even scary, and cause you to hesitate about moving persistently forward. In most cases, clouded mental focus and emotional reactions could be the recycling of some underlying, unconscious thoughts and feelings from your past—your blank spots.

To address blank spots that interfere with mental focus and emotional strength, the key is openness. The type of openness that brings change is rigorous, even deep from-the-heart honesty. Even your most "sacred" thoughts and feelings may come up for examination. Take a few moments to reflect on where you are with your personal honesty about your behaviors. Your life will then unfold in miraculous ways and you will find yourself living a life beyond your wildest dreams. Peace and harmony are just the beginning.

What to Expect

What you can expect will be many "aha!" moments as you acknowledge and look for the meaning of the challenges that have appeared. You will enter the flow of questions and answers, then more questions and answers. As you do your research with your inner detective and stay persistent throughout the process of addressing obstacles, you will find thoughts and feelings that resonate. This resonance is your mind and heart agreeing they have encountered part of your authentic self.

Let's explore the blank spots that can get in the way of mental focus and emotional strength.

View Life with Mental Focus and Emotional Strength—The Blank Spots

If you don't challenge yourself to clarify your thinking and feelings, especially those that interfere with reaching your goals, you may find yourself stuck with little growth or movement. These blank spots cause you to feel stuck. What are your thoughts and feelings around mistakes, control, boundaries, expectations in relationships, self-esteem, codependency, authenticity, taking care of yourself, or any aspect of your process toward reaching your goals?

The following exploration of blank spots will support you as you search for answers and understanding of how to Come Alive with mental focus and emotional strength.

EMOTIONAL STRENGTH

Do you live a reactionary life, going from one emotional charge to another from others' words or behaviors, or from events? Without a method to find calm and engage in some analysis with a clear mind, finding a measured response becomes difficult. Emotional strength comes from taking time to acknowledge how you are feeling and allowing yourself to still act on your goal.

Radical acceptance of your feelings, meaning you allow your feelings—whether positive, negative, or neutral—to flow through you without judgment is one of the most empowering tools you can have since you stop the inner fights over not wanting to feel your feelings. You then have the power and strength to do what you want to do. Emotional strength is part of the foundation of reaching every goal because you can keep moving forward, even if you have some doubts or fears.

My emotional eating only started to heal when it became clear to me feeling my feelings and becoming emotionally strong, as well as staying mentally focused on my goal, were two important pieces in that healing.

VISUALIZE THE END RESULT – MENTAL FOCUS

Mental focus includes seeing what you want your goal to look and feel like in as much detail as you can.

My favorite story illustrating visualization as mental focus is one that includes the DC Comics' character, The Flash. You know, that fellow who moves so fast he looks like a flame rocketing along at unbelievable speeds?

Being over seventy years old, some people might guess that if they were to see me walking cautiously. A physical therapist made it clear this physical weakness came from a weak core, and that fact had her close to recommending a cane. The good news, she said, was that strengthening my core muscles could correct the balance issues and eliminate the cautious walking.

My first challenge was in changing my limiting beliefs that weakness and balance issues were due to aging. Beginning with a visualization of myself running up the stairs to the second-floor apartment we then lived in seemed to be my answer to start to change that belief. My visualization exercise became a routine, especially before going to sleep. Visualization is what I consider a fun form of mental focus.

One night when I came home from a meeting, I realized if I didn't get upstairs to our bathroom I would thoroughly wet my pants. Darn that last yummy cup of coffee! Purse on my arm, grabbing both stair railings, I RAN up the stairs and into our bathroom. (Yes, I made it.)

Then I realized what I had done. I RAN! I wouldn't have even conceived of the thought of running upstairs before my visualization practice.

USE STRONG EMOTIONS

There is a story of a man who had a severe drinking problem. One day he simply had had enough of the terrible consequences he had experienced with his drinking. He gathered up all his bottles of booze and went out into the backyard. With all the emotion and passion he felt about quitting drinking, he smashed the bottles to pieces. Many years passed before he even thought of drinking again. The moral of this story is he used strong emotions that actually changed—rewired—his thinking. He moved beyond his emotional connection to the alcohol. He became emotionally strong.

If you want to make permanent changes in your life or manifest something, do like that man did and use strong emotions—positive affirmations, incantations, or mantras as a catalyst to change your thinking.

First, pick a positive statement your mind can accept. Then yell that out. Sing it out. However you do this, make those statements with strong, from-the-heart feelings. Driving in your car is a good place to talk out loud if you worry others will hear you. You might giggle or laugh or even cry. This is because you have just faced whatever emotional blank spots you have, and something from deep within has been released.

When you express your goals with strong emotion, you are telling your unconscious mind how extremely serious you are about what you want. This action will lead you to "aha!" moments right and left.

One clarification: If you are having self-esteem issues or a lot of doubts about yourself, this should be addressed before you use this technique on your goals. If those doubts and a poor self-image are deep enough, they might create an inner fight that isn't useful.

THE ULTIMATE RESPONSIBILITY IS YOURS

When you acknowledge and accept responsibility for your inner life and your reactions to your outer life, you support yourself to clear the way to reach any goal you desire. If you believe another person or multiple people, or past experiences, created the trouble in your life or have held you back in any way, your chance of changing, healing, or reaching your goal is limited. You may be stuck in some type of fear of being able to manage life yourself.

To understand this blank spot, start with focusing on what you feel is standing in the way of your success. If something you feel like you have no control over comes up, it's time to launch your inner detective to explore what may be baggage or unconscious messages from your past.

One thing I know for sure is when you are experiencing a sense of freedom in your choices, you have learned to deal with the fear of managing your life. That is the reward of being responsible.

EXERCISE #7

View Life with Mental Focus and Emotional Strength

This exercise will show you how having a daily focus and motivation will lead you to consistent mental focus and emotional strength.

In the book *The Compound Effect* by Darren Hardy, not only does Hardy suggest how small changes and choices can change your destiny, he gives you a great model of morning and evening practices.

Do some reflecting on what might lift you up in the morning as you schedule your day. Then, in the evening, regroup and celebrate your accomplishments or failures so you can learn from them. This not only gets you focused on your day's activities, it helps you feel your feelings of success or failure and know you will be able to move on, having grown wiser. Be open to changing your practices. See if you then start to experience clearer mental focus and stronger emotions.

Questions for Reflection

- Do you question your thinking or conclusions? Does your thinking feel right on, or are you led to believe you require some further exploration?
- How do you manage your emotions when you are facing a problem? Are you able to feel negative emotions and still do what you want to do?
- Do you frequently have "aha!" moments that help you find clarity?
- Are you strong enough to see your reactions for what they are—past baggage?
- Have you learned that the *how* of reaching a goal is not as important as visualizing and feeling the feelings of the result?
- Have you discovered how having strong emotions attached to a goal speeds up success?
- Have you made excuses for failing to achieve your goals, or do you take responsibility, see the failure as feedback, and learn what you may not understand so you can move on?
- How did you feel about this chapter?

Summary

When you have cleared the way to find what it takes to be

mentally focused and emotionally strong, you have the two greatest resources for coming alive in your toolbox. You discover you have an attitude of "if I can conceive it, I can do it."

CHAPTER EIGHT

Step Five—
Experience the Change

"Creating a change is only a small part of making the change permanent; the bigger part is to learn to live in the change comfortably."

CORALEE KULMAN

Experience a New World with Change

Now that you've made changes, perhaps your life feels "off." Self-doubt may start to haunt you. People you usually enjoy being around may start to bug you.

These could be signals you are in a period of change or you have been successful with a goal and have moved into the unknown world of new awareness that change has brought. You may be facing a period of adjustment as you become comfortable living in your new success.

Yes, the change you wanted might alter your world as you once knew it. This is like going into a new area on a trip: you may need to adjust to the new environment. However, if you know what to expect, your adjustment won't take long, and it is so worth the effort to make the change permanent.

What to Expect

Of course, experiencing success and change will be different for everyone. However, odds are, one feeling you might experience is that of vulnerability. *Merriam-Webster* defines vulnerability as: "capable of being physically or emotionally wounded and open to attack or damage."

If you haven't watched Brene' Brown's TED talk on vulnerability, please do. She outlines how successful people know vulnerability is part of the path to success. If you experience the symptoms of vulnerability—hesitation to move forward, butterflies in your stomach, or outright fear—view that as a sign you are succeeding.

Knowing that you may experience feelings of vulnerability during change is a sure way to become emotionally strong enough to see yourself move through those moments.

Experience Change—The Blank Spots

Following is an exploration of the blank spots that hinder change and, thus, hinder coming alive. When you make changes and experience life at its fullest, knowledge of your blank spots will be the springboard.

When you experience change, you are witnessing how blank spots, obstacles, problems, and challenges show up and lead you through the ebb and flow of life and your growth. When you mindfully travel through the experience of change and take it all in, you are learning what the fullness of life offers. Let's explore those areas to see if you have any blank spots that might hinder your journey.

"AHA!" MOMENTS

In the last chapter, we talked about how to expect "aha!" moments when you start to search for clarity in your thinking and emotions. "Aha!" moments also begin to support a structure you will see as your authentic self. Here is a little more about "aha!" moments to provide clarity in case you think you don't have "aha!" moments.

"Aha!" moments are the most valuable feedback you can get. They are when the mind and heart connect in a real demonstration of the harmony between your of body, mind, and spirit. They signal growth and movement. They are the measuring stick of when you have found a new piece in coming alive.

Sometimes called the eureka effect, insight, inspiration, epiphany, paradigm shift, light-bulb moment, or sudden realization—an "aha!" moment rings true, answers a question, or solves a problem. Usually, these moments are sudden and easy to incorporate into your awareness. If you think you aren't having any "aha!" moments, turn experiencing an "aha!" moment into a goal itself.

FEELINGS—WHERE CHANGE CAN START

Nestled in the middle of this chapter is probably the most important bit of information in this book. Here it is in one sentence: The key to change comes from the ability to know how you feel, not just what you think. Another way to put it is "change comes from knowing what is in your heart as well as knowing what you want."

Movement out of this lack of acceptance of your feelings is where manifesting the things you want in your life starts. Your "thinking nature" is your guide, and your "feeling nature" is your strongest motivator to persist through the challenges that come up until you reach your goal.

To begin to address and eliminate this blank spot, pay attention to what you are feeling. Notice each feeling and even label it: joy, sadness, fear, anger, disgust, surprise, trust, etc. Then slow down and experience any of these feelings that come up until you know you will recognize what's going on when one of these feelings shows up again.

This process will help you become more emotionally strong

by teaching you how to experience your feelings without having to react. In slowing down, you can also learn to not judge your feelings and even develop a strategy to manage your feelings with measured responses.

PERSISTENCE

Persistence is sometimes called discipline or willpower. Essentially, it is a time in your journey toward your goal when something may come up that seems to thwart your path to success. You may doubt yourself, or even feel like a failure, because it has become so difficult. The true cause is you have a blank spot, or a series of blank spots, that are interfering with your persistence.

Often, I talk about digging deeper. In this situation, it may be time to set an additional goal of learning what blank spot is getting in your way. Start your inner detective work. Think about the feelings you are feeling and see if you can remember the first time you felt that way. Awareness can help you master your lack of persistence. Be persistent in your goals, be open to the road ahead, and you will find yourself saying, "I reach every goal I set."

LIVE YOUR SUCCESS

You have arrived. Time for a victory dance! Now your only task is to get used to the change and practice reinforcing your new way of living. Start by enjoying the experience. Immerse yourself in the great feelings you now feel. Some people actually try to keep from being excited because they think getting too excited might jinx their newly discovered happiness—a blank spot in itself.

One thing that helps you enjoy the success phase in your life is knowing there will always be more growth and change ahead. That is a big part of what coming alive means.

EXERCISE #8

Success is the Challenge

If you find you resist enjoying your success, then find a way to embrace and experience what it is like to be successful.

Have a celebration party and invite your friends. Do a daily celebration post on Facebook or in your journal. Do a daily evening regroup of your day and consciously express gratitude to yourself for being successful.

Watch to see if this practice doesn't make success a welcome part of your Come-Alive life.

Questions for Reflection

- Have you ever wondered what your time-to-change signals are?
- Did you expect success could cause you to feel vulnerable or confused?
- Do you frequently have "aha!" moments and a sense of movement in your life?

- Where are you with your feelings? Do you know the importance of being aware of your feelings in coming alive?
- When you are successful with your goals or intentions, do you know how to manage the awkwardness of the new world you just stepped into? How does this look?
- What do you do to celebrate your successes?
- How did this chapter feel to you?

Summary

Success is stepping into another world, and for a while you may feel awkward or even a little vulnerable or unsafe. There are people who may back-step into old ways because of this awkwardness or vulnerability. However, when you know what to expect, you will be empowered to move through this period and make the positive changes permanent.

We get all excited and motivated about building our business, getting thin and fit, finding a new love, and just plain becoming successful in whatever our passion is. We are motivated as we overcome the challenges to reach our goals. Then success comes. What then? Does this feel absolutely fantastic, or is there some awkwardness about living in this new, changed world? Knowing what to expect will make all your changes and growth feel fantastic.

CHAPTER NINE

Conclusion

"Once you master the process of creating a richer, happier life, you have mastered everything you need to know to Come Alive. You will live a life of joy, peace, and fulfilment. Doesn't get any better than that."

CORALEE KULMAN

Challenges and Change Are the Magic of Life

You may think stability, consistency, and steadiness are the foundation of a good life. You may be surprised to find I disagree. Well, maybe not disagree as much as believe these are only the *beginning* of a good life. After achieving stability, consistency, and steadiness to help you Come Alive, you must also add creativity, innovation, vulnerability, and courage. When you add these characteristics to your experience of life, you have all the internal resources to Come Alive.

Take another look at the change process we talked about:

A – Acknowledge your issue or problem and ask for what you want

L – Launch your inner detective to research information needed for change.

I – Initiate your personal solution-finding process to help you face the challenges that change can bring.

V – View your life experiences and obstacles with mental focus and emotional strength.

E – Experience the change through knowing what to expect and how to practice making that change a part of your new life.

These steps will serve you well in helping you to reach any goal or intention you set for yourself. They are life affirming on many levels.

You will see challenges not as obstacles stopping you from what you want, but as containing the answers you're looking for and, thus, the seeds of transformational information.

You will learn to acknowledge your moods and the times

when you feel off as signals to dig a little deeper to find new information to help you understand what you're feeling.

You will know exactly what to do when you have a decision to make or a problem to solve.

You will be mentally focused and emotionally strong—the winning combination to move you forward toward your goals.

Last, but not least, you will be comfortable and flexible as the change your goals bring becomes a part of a fantastic, Come-Alive world you now live in.

What's Ahead

BOOK TWO

Come Alive: The Components of Coming Alive

This book delves into the many unconscious blank spots so prevalent in our society and world today. They are the cause of the conflicts we see and experience. Once you understand what it's like to have emotional strength, mental focus, physical well-being, spiritual living, political awareness, relationship connection skills, and manifesting, you will have all the components of coming alive.

The journey you will find yourself on will encourage you to find what fits for you. Best of all, you will be at peace and confident you can get through whatever life presents to you.

When you have come to your personal positions on these components through your exploration, you will have created the structure of your identity, making it unshakeable in difficult times and filling you with the confidence that you can master whatever you face.

BOOK THREE

Come Alive: Create Awesome Relationships

When all is said and done, it's your successful relationships—including the one with yourself—that is instrumental in a Come-Alive life. If you find relationships perplexing, this book gives you the information on the blank spots that are getting in the way.

Time to set aside your resentments, disappointments, and unfulfilled connections and replace them with confidence, intimacy, and love. Oh, yes, and success.

Gifts for You

Understanding and mastering your life means the sky's the limit. Ask yourself, "What dreams have I put off, or let go of, because they seemed too complex?" Let your dreams float up, then embrace every challenge that comes your way. That's how you will Come Alive.

Few people can do this alone. Would you like to see what happens when you're part of a like-minded and compassionate group that supports you on your journey? Go to my website at **www.coraleekulman.com** for a way to connect with me and those like-minded travelers as well as see articles and other useful information and resources.

Isn't it time you invest in yourself? You're worth it.

ABOUT THE AUTHOR

Coralee Kulman

A joyful discovery came when I learned that life's challenges can bring "aha!" moments and move me into a whole new awareness, or wisdom. I wanted to live there forever. Then came a new challenge and another "aha!" moment. Wow! More love and wisdom. My discovery became what I describe as coming alive.

Come Alive came from a deeply personal mission to find the meaning of love and how to express it. Since love is an experience of sharing, my discovery led to my writing and connecting with you all. This is who I am and why I do what I do.

APPENDIX A

Exercise List Index

APPENDIX B

More Questions

"Questions are one of the most effective tools in any challenge you face. Form the question and you are 95% closer to the answer."

CORALEE KULMAN

Here are additional questions for you. Go for it and dig a little deeper, dear reader . . .

YOUR PERSONAL STORY

- Do you have a legacy, one you are proud of?
- Do you believe it is too late to get what you want out of life?
- Do you see your life full of bad luck or good luck?
- Do you feel different than everyone you know?
- Are you bored with your life? Is it always the same old, same old?

- Do you never seem to catch a break?
- Do you struggle because you are gay, black, Hispanic, Muslim or ????
- Do you wonder if life is anything more than just a pain in the behind?
- Did you do poorly in school and that makes you feel stupid to this day?
- Do you think you need to solve all your problems before you take good care of yourself?

PROBLEMS

- What is the most pressing challenge in your life now?
- Do you feel having problems is caused from being weak or stupid?
- Do you want to give up when it feels like you are hit by one problem after another?
- Are your problems always crisis-type situations?
- Do you avoid thinking about a problem, even if it requires you to make a decision soon?

CHANGE

- Have you given any thought about how you can

make changes in your life or do you just wing it in every situation?

- What tools do you use to make changes?
- Can you make changes even if doing so becomes difficult?

EMOTIONAL STRENGTH

- Does the thought of touchy, feely stuff repel you?
- Do you feel angry, depressed, or fearful most of the time?
- Do you have others tell you that you have an anger problem?
- Do you not feel safe if you are not in control?
- Do you hate it when someone asks you, “What’s the matter?”
- Are you weighed down with worry?
- Do you freak out or have emotional outbursts?
- Do unsettled feelings cause you to want to distract or numb yourself?
- Is it hard for you to share your true feelings, even with people you love?
- Do you or any of your family members have addictions?

MENTAL FOCUS

- Do you over-analyze and feel you are going in circles with no answers?
- Do you sometimes think you obsess over things?
- Do you sometimes feel you are losing your mind?
- Do you fight yourself over what to do and not do?

YOUR SHADOW SIDE

- Are there mistakes you have made that you cannot forgive yourself for?
- Do you have nightmares from the past?
- Is your first reaction to things to see the problems or why something won't work?
- Do you have an ex you actively try to disconnect from your children?
- Have you been abused by anyone?
- Are you suspicious of everyone?
- Have you hit someone in anger?
- Do you not trust yourself to say no to sexual advances?
- Do you automatically think you are wrong during confrontations?

- Do you have obsessive-compulsive behaviors like washing and cleaning, counting, checking, demanding reassurances, having to have things orderly and symmetrical, trichotillomania, skin picking, cutting, or ?????
- Do you fight with yourself over what you consider your weaknesses?

PHYSICAL WELL-BEING

- Do you notice there are places in your body you feel tension or stress?
- Are you always in physical pain?
- Do you have a lot of stress?
- Are you out of shape?
- Do you hate your body?
- Have you done drugs, smoked, purged, or done other things that cause you to be concerned about the possibility you may have harmed your body?
- Do you have some serious, even life-threatening illness or disease?
- Do you feel vulnerable without your fat?
- Does stress contribute to your high blood pressure, asthma, obesity, diabetes, headaches, depression,

anxiety, gastrointestinal problems, and accelerated aging?

- Do you have one illness after another?
- Do you try to lose weight, or gain weight, and fail?

SPIRITUAL LIVING

- Do you believe in a higher power or presence or universal laws?
- Do you feel organized religion is sheep following sheep?
- Has your spirituality confused you?
- Have you prayed to God and did not get what you had prayed for?
- Are you rebelling against religion because it was forced on you as a young person?
- Has your relationship with God let you down or enhanced your life?
- Do you believe you are right and others are wrong about certain religious issues and they must be led to change?
- Do you see tolerance as a weakness?
- Has your church caused you to feel disillusioned?

POLITICAL AWARENESS

- Does the way you see us as a nation environmentally, politically, financially give you concern?
- Do you believe all politicians are corrupt?
- Does the political rhetoric confuse you?
- How much do you understand about the constitution?
- How much do you understand about the balance of powers?
- Do you believe you are right, others are wrong, and they need to change?
- Do you believe tolerance is a weakness?

Relationship Connection Skills

CONFLICT

- Have you explored what conflict is?
- Have you explored the benefits of conflict?

THE MEANING OF LOVE AND HOW TO COMMUNICATE IT

- Do you give as much as you take?

- Do you look suspiciously at potential problems when you meet someone?
- Are you hesitant to share concerns you have?
- Is romance a foreign word to you?
- Can you express your love with more than material gifts?
- Do you have trouble when you are told you are wrong or misunderstood?
- Do you feel uncomfortable sharing your deep feelings for someone?
- Does loving another person feel like it means you have lost who you are as an individual?
- Do you feel you are being heard?
- Do you think you are hearing your partner or spouse?
- Do you stumble when you try to express what is on your mind and heart?

PERSONAL RELATIONSHIPS

- Do you have people who you have been alienated from for years?
- Are you introverted or shy to the point it interferes with your relationships?

- Do you have one broken relationship after another and aren't sure why?
- Do you struggle with the people you work with?
- Do you think most people just don't get you?
- Do you rebel about what you view as societal norms?
- Are you distressed if people disagree with you?
- Do you expect the worst from people?
- Do you feel put down by others a lot?
- Do you isolate frequently?
- Do you have relationships you lean on a lot?
- Do you allow yourself to talk about others' failings, even giggle about them and feel you are better than they are?
- Do you feel alienated from, or uncomfortable with, society in general?
- Are you uncomfortable in groups or parties?
- Do you have few close friends?
- Are people unkind to you about your race, culture, sexual orientation, or religion?
- Do you struggle with people who are different?

- Have you judged others, or have you been judged?

PARENTS AND FAMILY

- Do you feel like the black sheep in your family?
- Are you embarrassed by some of your family members' behaviors, lifestyle, and attitudes?
- Does your family reject you?
- Do you have major philosophical, religious, or political differences that cause conflict with family?
- Were you physically, emotionally, or sexually abused by a parent or family member?

CHILDREN

- Do you and your spouse or partner have conflicts over how to raise your children?
- Do you doubt your ability to parent?
- Are your children respectful?
- Are your children stuck in an addiction?
- Do your children get into a lot of trouble?

MARRIAGE AND PARTNERS

- Is intimacy a problem?

- Do you fight a lot without resolution?
- Do you or your spouse/partner make every fight a big deal to be right about?
- Do you have date nights or scheduled times together?
- Is money an issue for you and your spouse/partner?
- Do you have opposite goals from those of your spouse/partner?
- Is your sexual relationship pleasurable?
- Are you gay or transgender and hesitant to tell others?
- Has coming out caused you a lot of trouble or rejection?
- Are there areas in your marriage or partnership that bother you and you have accepted they may not change and resent this?

MANIFESTING

- Do you reach every goal you set?
- Do you take failure personally, as if you are defective in some way?
- Are you living in an area that stresses you?

- Is your house chronically messy?
- Do you make good money, yet debt imprisons you?
- When you come into some extra money, does something always break, need replacement or repair, and you use up all your spare money?
- Are you chronically unemployed or underemployed?
- Does money feel like "the root of evil" to you?
- Do you resent your job?
- Are you artistic and struggle to make a living doing what you love?
- Are you in a dead-end job?
- Are you mistreated at your work?
- Do you make a lot of mistakes at your job?
- Is your home environment a sanctuary or a prison?
- Are you living on the edge financially?

YOUR AUTHENTIC SELF

- Do you feel you are too dependent on someone else, or do you give up some of your own needs because you are afraid of losing the other person?
- Do you have free time to pursue your interests?

- Do you lose yourself when you are around others and forget who you really are?
- Do you feel you can't be alone, that you always need someone around?
- Do you have more resentments than gratitude?
- Do you wonder who you really are?
- Are you fearful of revealing yourself completely?
- Are you always so concerned about others that you forget to express your own needs?
- Do you think speaking your truth might be too harsh or hurt another person's feelings?
- Do you know what is holding you back from being authentic?
- Do you know if you are having a fight that you are addressing the real issues?

YOUR PURPOSE

- Do you have multiple interests and purposes?
- Do you have a passion for something that feels like a purpose for you?
- Are you hesitant to pursue your passion or purpose because you believe it might change your life too much?

- Has a job or family responsibilities been given priority over your passion or purpose?
- Are there ways to enjoy your interests in spite of your responsibilities? What would they be?
- Do you have a passion for something, but don't take time to pursue this interest?

FAILING

- Do you feel failing is a sign you are going in the wrong direction or your goal isn't right for you?
- Do you hesitate to try something because of how people might react if you fail?

WHY COME ALIVE?

- Are you motivated to persevere until you reach your goals?
- Do you think you are not destined to Come Alive?

I am sure there are plenty of other thoughtful questions that can be added. Send any of your own to me if you'd like to do so. You can contact me using this link:

www.coraleekulman.com/contact

Acknowledgements

To my mastermind friends, Marie Stewart, Maribeth Slovasky, and Kenny Mack who have been instrumental in my personal and business growth and successes.

To Heidi whose friendship and support in our mutual journey to coming alive has been enlightening and full of laughter.

To my good friend, Julia, who has come in and out of my life at just the right times. Together we've manifested miracles.

Made in the USA
Columbia, SC
14 September 2021